Moose

Victoria Blakemore

Table of Contents

What Are Moose?

Moose are large mammals. They are the largest members of the deer family.

There are four kinds of moose in North America. They differ in size, color, and where they live. The moose that live in Europe are often called elk.

Moose can be many different shades of brown. Males are usually darker than females.

Size

Moose can grow to be over six feet tall. Adults can weigh over 1,000 pounds. The largest moose on record weighed 1,800 pounds.

Male moose are called bulls. They can be twice the size of female moose.

Female moose are called cows. They are usually smaller than bulls.

Physical Characteristics

Moose have a thick coat of fur that helps to keep them warm in the winter. In the summer, they rub on trees to remove the extra fur.

Moose have long legs. This helps them to wade through water and walk in the snow.

6

Moose have a flap of skin on their neck. It is called a bell. Researchers are not sure what it is used for.

Antlers

Bulls have large antlers on their head. They are also called paddles. They can use them to fight other bulls.

Moose antlers are covered in velvet. As the antlers grow, moose rub them on trees to rub the velvet off. Antlers can weigh over fifty pounds.

Bulls shed their antlers each year in the winter. They grow bigger antlers each spring.

Habitat

Moose are found in forests.

They are often seen around

the water. Rivers, marshes,

and lakes provide moose with

water and food like willows.

It can get very cold where

moose live. Their thick fur helps

to keep them warm.

Range

Moose are found in the northern parts of Europe, Asia, and North America.

Canada is home to more moose

than any other country.

Diet

Moose are **herbivores**. They only eat plants. They have been known to eat up to 73 pounds of plants each day!

Their diet is made up of grasses, shrubs, willows, moss, lichen, and twigs.

Moose prefer to eat taller plants so that they don't have to bend down as far.

In the winter, moose use their large hooves to scrape the snow away from the ground so they can look for food like mosses or lichen.

Their hooves also help them to walk in the snow or mud. The size of the hooves stops them from sinking in.

Food can be hard to find in the winter. Moose have to eat whatever they can find.

Communication

Moose make many different sounds to communicate with each other. They can bark, bellow, croak, and grunt.

Moose that are **agitated** make a snort noise. It is used to warn whatever is bothering them. They have been known to attack people and animals.

Mother have a special grunt

that they use to communicate

with their calves.

Movement

Moose can run up to thirty-five miles per hour for short distances. They are often seen trotting at about twenty miles per hour.

Moose spend much of their day **grazing**. They are always looking for places with plenty of food.

Moose are good swimmers.

They can swim to cross rivers.

They can stay underwater for

about thirty seconds.

Solitary Life

Moose are usually **solitary**. They spend most of their time alone.

More than one moose may be looking for food in the same area, but they often ignore each other.

Moose are not usually seen in a group. When they are, their group is called a herd.

Moose Calves

Moose have one or two babies in the spring. They are called calves and weigh about thirty pounds when they are born.

Calves stay with their mother for about a year and a half. Then, they are old enough to go off on their own.

Mothers help their calves by

protecting them from predators.

Life Span

In the wild, moose often live between fifteen and twenty-five years.

The main threats that moose face are disease and **parasites** such as winter ticks.

Once moose are fully

grown, they are usually safe

from predators.

Population

Moose are not in danger of becoming **extinct**. There are thought to be over one million moose in North America.

Moose populations have been **declining** in some areas. This may be because of habitat destruction and hunting.

Helping Moose

People are trying to help moose so that they do not become **endangered**.

Moose crossing signs are put along roads where moose are known to cross. They warn drivers to watch for moose on the road.

People hunt moose for food or sport. There are laws to protect moose from **overhunting**.

Rising temperatures are causing problems for moose. There are more parasites and moose have been getting sick. People want to try to stop the rising temperatures to help animals like moose.

Glossary

Agitated: upset or annoyed

Declining: getting smaller

Endangered: at risk of becoming

extinct

Extinct: when there are no more

of an animal left alive

Grazing: feeding on growing

grass and plants

Herbivore: an animal that eats

only plants

Overhunting: when too many of

an animal are hunted

Predators: animals that hunt and

eat other animals

Parasite: a plant or animal that

feeds on the energy of another

animal

Solitary: living alone

About the Author

Victoria Blakemore is a first grade

teacher in Southwest Florida with a

passion for reading.

You can visit her at

www.elementaryexplorers.com

Also in This Series

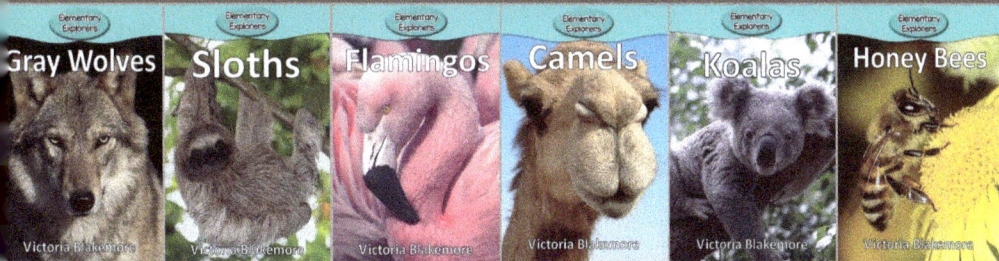

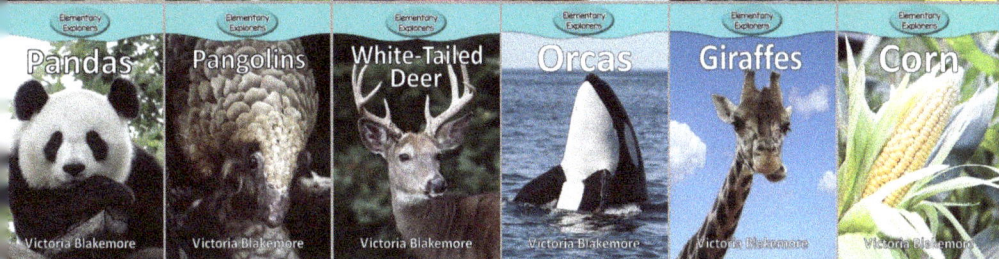

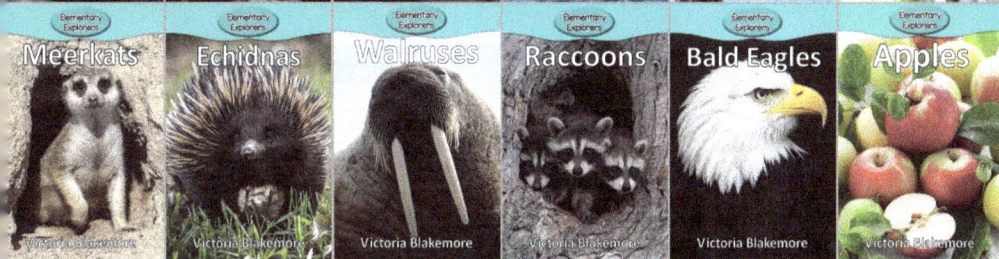

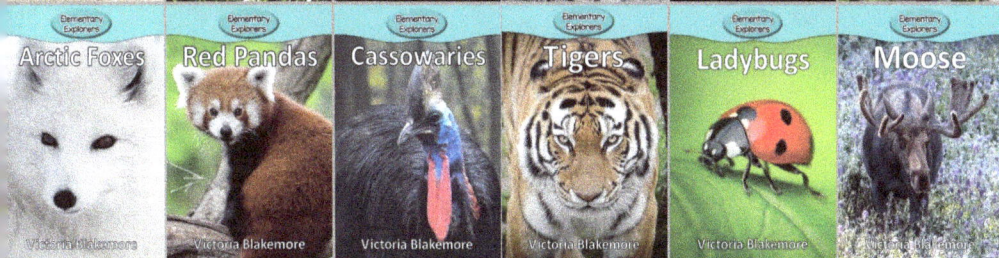

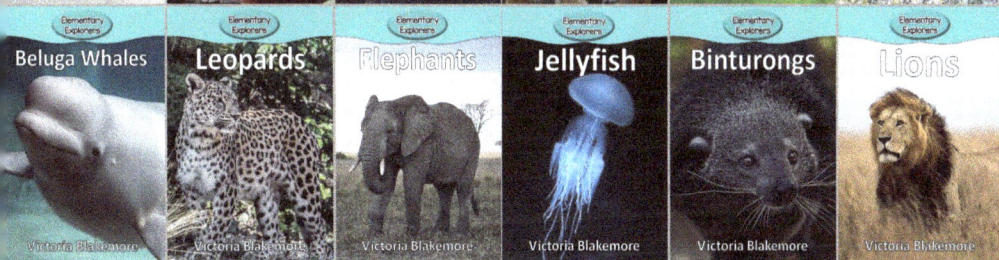

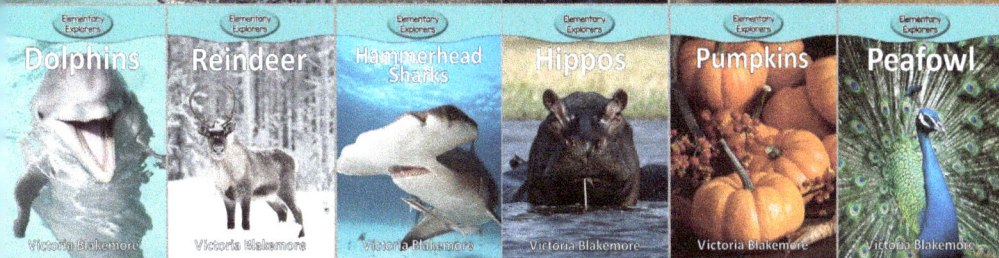

Elementary Explorers **Gray Wolves** Victoria Blakemore	Elementary Explorers **Sloths** Victoria Blakemore	Elementary Explorers **Flamingos** Victoria Blakemore	Elementary Explorers **Camels** Victoria Blakemore	Elementary Explorers **Koalas** Victoria Blakemore	Elementary Explorers **Honey Bees** Victoria Blakemore
Elementary Explorers **Pandas** Victoria Blakemore	Elementary Explorers **Pangolins** Victoria Blakemore	Elementary Explorers **White-Tailed Deer** Victoria Blakemore	Elementary Explorers **Orcas** Victoria Blakemore	Elementary Explorers **Giraffes** Victoria Blakemore	Elementary Explorers **Corn** Victoria Blakemore
Elementary Explorers **Meerkats** Victoria Blakemore	Elementary Explorers **Echidnas** Victoria Blakemore	Elementary Explorers **Walruses** Victoria Blakemore	Elementary Explorers **Raccoons** Victoria Blakemore	Elementary Explorers **Bald Eagles** Victoria Blakemore	Elementary Explorers **Apples** Victoria Blakemore
Elementary Explorers **Arctic Foxes** Victoria Blakemore	Elementary Explorers **Red Pandas** Victoria Blakemore	Elementary Explorers **Cassowaries** Victoria Blakemore	Elementary Explorers **Tigers** Victoria Blakemore	Elementary Explorers **Ladybugs** Victoria Blakemore	Elementary Explorers **Moose** Victoria Blakemore
Elementary Explorers **Beluga Whales** Victoria Blakemore	Elementary Explorers **Leopards** Victoria Blakemore	Elementary Explorers **Elephants** Victoria Blakemore	Elementary Explorers **Jellyfish** Victoria Blakemore	Elementary Explorers **Binturongs** Victoria Blakemore	Elementary Explorers **Lions** Victoria Blakemore
Elementary Explorers **Dolphins** Victoria Blakemore	Elementary Explorers **Reindeer** Victoria Blakemore	Elementary Explorers **Hammerhead Sharks** Victoria Blakemore	Elementary Explorers **Hippos** Victoria Blakemore	Elementary Explorers **Pumpkins** Victoria Blakemore	Elementary Explorers **Peafowl** Victoria Blakemore

Also in This Series

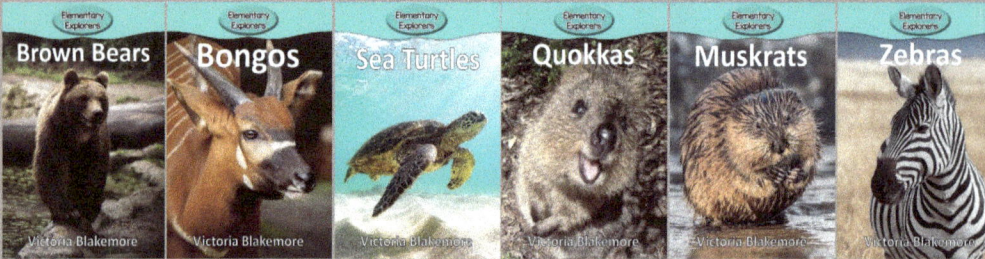

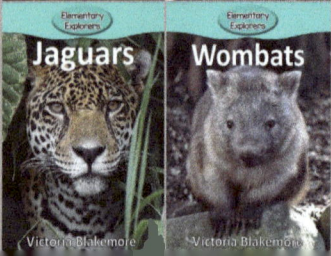

Chameleons	**Florida Panthers**	**Aye-Ayes**	**Black Bears**	**Cheetahs**	**Manatees**
Gingerbread	**Polar Bears**	**Hot Chocolate**	**Orangutans**	**Coyotes**	**Marshmallow**
Strawberries	**Aardvarks**	**Mako Sharks**	**Alligators**	**Frogs**	**Hedgehogs**
Brown Bears	**Bongos**	**Sea Turtles**	**Quokkas**	**Muskrats**	**Zebras**
Red Foxes	**Ring-Tailed Lemurs**	**Platypuses**	**Anteaters**	**Kangaroos**	**Rhinos**
Jaguars	**Wombats**				

Each title:
Elementary Explorers — Victoria Blakemore

www.ingramcontent.com/pod-product-compliance
Lightning Source LLC
Chambersburg PA
CBHW051252020426
42333CB00025B/3179